George Hempl

Old-English phonology

George Hempl

Old-English phonology

ISBN/EAN: 9783741131806

Manufactured in Europe, USA, Canada, Australia, Japa

Cover: Foto ©Thomas Meinert / pixelio.de

Manufactured and distributed by brebook publishing software (www.brebook.com)

George Hempl

Old-English phonology

OLD-ENGLISH PHONOLOGY

BY

GEORGE HEMPL, Ph.D.

ASSISTANT PROFESSOR OF ENGLISH IN THE
UNIVERSITY OF MICHIGAN

BOSTON U. S. A.
D. C. HEATH & CO.
1893

COPYRIGHT
D. C. HEATH & CO.
1892

NOTE.

The following pages are the first of my forthcoming *Old-English Grammar and Reader*. They are now published primarily for the use of the members of my classes.

It is expected that the complete book will be issued in the summer of 1893; at which time due acknowledgments will be made to books and friends.

GEORGE HEMPL.

Ann Arbor,
Oct., 1892.

SIGNS AND ABBREVIATIONS.

$>$ = "become(s)," "became," or "(is changed) into."
$<$ = "(derived) from," "a later form of."
* marks a form not found in Mss. but inferred philologically.
/ is a sign of gradation, § 47.
⫶ is a sign of the working of Verner's Law, § 57.
$+$ = "plus," or "together with following."
⌈ = "after," or "preceded by," for ex., ʷ⌈$io > u$ = "io after w becomes u," or "under the influence of a preceding w, an io becomes u."
⌉ = "before," or "followed by," for ex., e⌉ⁿᵃˢ· $> i$ = "e before a nasal, becomes i."
⌐ = "breaks," or "broken," § 41, for ex., i⌐ $> io$ = "i breaks into io," or "breaking changes i to io," and $ea < æ$⌐ = "the ea that arises by the breaking of $æ$."
)ⁱ = "i-mutation," § 43;)ᵘ = "u-mutation," § 44. For ex., $ō$)ⁱ $> ē$ = "the i-mutation of $ō$ is $ē$," or "$ō$ mutated by i becomes $ē$."

$ā, ē$, &c., § 15 N².
$ĉ, ġ, ḣ$, &c., § 85.
$ę, į$, § 40 N³.
$ę, ǫ$, ft. nt. p. 22, § 38.
χ = the voiceless fricatives in German ach (back) and ich (front), § 54.
ü = a sound like i in 'machine' or 'pin,' but made with the lips nearly closed, or "rounded."

$i̯, u̯$, &c. = "unsyllabic i, u, &c."
η = the back nasal in 'sing,' § 53.
ʃ = sh in 'she.'
ʒ = s in 'pleasure.'

eWS.	= early West Saxon, § 7.	N.E.	= New England.
Gᶜ	= Germanic, § 6.	OE.	= Old English, §§ 8, 9.
lWS.	= late West Saxon, § 7.	OHG.	= Old High German, § 6.
ME.	= Middle English, § 9.	Sc.	= Scandinavian, § 6.
M. Ger.	= Midland German.	S. Ger.	= South German.
MⁿE.	= Modern English, § 9.	WG.	= West Germanic, § 6.
N	= Note.	WS.	= West Saxon, § 7.

INTRODUCTION.

THE LAND AND THE PEOPLE.*

1. ENGLAND, once a peninsula like Denmark, had been separated from the mainland long before the first tribes of Indo-European stock came and conquered the people they found there. These new-comers were **Celts**, and had become thoroughly established on the island when Cæsar, having conquered the Celts of Gaul, invaded Britain with his Roman legions, 55 and again 54 B.C. The **Roman conquest**, however, did not begin until a century later, A.D. 43. In time forts arose in various parts; two immense walls were built to shut out the Picts of the north; and the island was traversed by great military roads, along which troops might quickly be sent to the west to hold the less civilized natives in restraint, to the north against the Scots and the Picts, or to the south-east to oppose the marauding Saxons that devastated that coast. But it is a mistake to suppose that Britain was only a military colony. Archæological and philological evidence is constantly accumulating to the effect that during the four hundred years of Roman rule Roman civilization not only pervaded the towns, but even spread to the country parts; in time **Christianity** gained a footing on the island. But large tracts were still covered by dense forests, and many rivers were not easily

---

* The learner is advised to read the first chapters of some good English history: Gardiner's Student's History; Green's History; Freeman's Old English History or vol. i. of his Norman Conquest.

approached for the great marshes that lined them. Little is recorded of the history of the Roman Province of Britain; after 410 Rome hardly claimed it, and no longer pretended to do for it.

2. The Saxon pirates were but the forerunners of a great **German invasion**, which began about 450 and in time overran the larger part of the island. The invaders were, for the most part, **Angles, Saxons**, and **Jutes** (OE. *Eṅġ-le, Se'axe* or *-an, Ī'ote*). Kent and the country about Southampton fell into the hands of the Jutes, the rest of the South was settled by Saxons, while the north-east became the home of the Angles. 'As it was among the *Eṅġle* of Northumberland that literary culture first flourished (§ 12) and an *Eṅġlisċ* dialect was the first to be used for vernacular literature, **Eṅġlisċ** came eventually to be a general name for all forms of the vernacular as opposed to Latin (which the English called *Læden*), etc.; and when the West Saxon of Ælfred became in its turn the literary or classical form of speech (§ 7), it too was called *Eṅġlisċ*, or English.'* Later the term **Angelcyn** (= Angle kin, or English people) came to be applied to Saxons as well as Angles, and the fact that the Angles occupied the larger part of the country may have had something to do with this. According to ancient usage, the words *Eṅġle* and *Angelcyn* were also used where we should expect a name for the country; but in time **Eṅġlaland** (MⁿE. *England*), that is, "land of the Engle," came into use. The natives, on their part, called all the new-comers by the name of those that first devastated their coast,—the Saxons. Many of these natives (the English called them **Welsh**, that is, "strangers") were either slain or driven to the west and the north, but not a few became the slaves of the conquerors, and their young women the mothers of a large part of the next generation. Thus, from the start, Celtic blood mingled with Teutonic.

* Murray in *Encyclopædia Britannica*.

3. The new-comers cared little for Roman civilization and Christianity, but brought with them the institutions, customs, and religion of their forefathers. The bulk of the free population consisted of **Ćeorls** (pronounce *kĕ'orls* or *chĕ'orls*), who in time sank to the position of serfs, and their betters, the **Eorls** (*ĕ'orls*) and **Æthelings** (*ădh'elings*). The chiefs were called **Ealdormen** (*ă'ŏldormen'*, = elders or magistrates) or **Her'etog'as** (= leaders of the army). Their retinue of fighting-men, called **Ġesīths** (*yĕ-seeths'*, = companions) and later **Thegns** (*thanes*, or attendants), was for the most part made up of Eorls. By those of lower rank an Ealdorman or a king was in deference called **Hlāford** (*hlah'vord*, Mⁿ E. *lord*). The general levy of the villagers for the defence of their homes was termed the **Fierd** (*fi'erd*). When various tribes united, as for a military expedition or for defence against a common foe, they chose a leader of the combined forces, whom they called **Cyning** (*küning*, = king); in time the kingship acquired more permanence and power, and supplanted or subordinated the rule of the Ealdormen. When a king was to be elected, the most eligible member of the royal family was chosen by the **Wit'enagemōt'** (*g = y*), an assembly or Great Council that to a certain extent controlled the action of the king. At times one king got a sort of supremacy over other kings and was called **Bretwealda** (*brĕt'wă'ŏlda*, = wielder of Britain), or overlord.

4. The history of England during the Old-English period (to about the twelfth century) is too full to be more than hinted at here. For a time Æth'elberht, king of Kent, was over-lord over the other kings south of the Humber; he married a Christian woman, the daughter of the king of the Franks, and permitted the establishment of **Christianity** among his people. Later, E'adwine, king of Northumberland and over-lord of all England except Kent, did the same. Gradually Christianity spread throughout the English domains, and there was a united English church before a united

England. There were three chief kingdoms: **Northumberland** (OE. *Norð-hymbre*, cf. Ẹngle, § 2, end, = those dwelling north of the Humber), **Mercia** (*mersha*, OE. *Mi'erċe* = the inhabitants of the *Mearc* or borderland), and **Wessex** (OE. *West Seaxe*, or the West Saxons); the over-lordship shifting to and fro.

5. About three hundred years (A.D. 787) after the first Teutonic hordes gained a footing on the island, others, called "**Danes**" by the English, but coming from the Scandinavian as well as from the Danish peninsula, began to make inroads upon the north-east coast. In time they founded settlements, and pressed forward until they were masters of most of the English territory north of the Thames. **Wessex** (with its dependencies, Sussex and Kent) alone held out against them. The West-Saxon resistance was maintained by a line of valiant kings, the greatest of whom was **Ælfred** (reigned 871–901), equally noted as warrior, statesman, and scholar. He consolidated his kingdom, reorganized the Fierd (§ 3), built a navy, had the laws revised, established schools, encouraged native scholars and attracted foreign ones, and, though his own knowledge of Latin was defective, translated with the aid of others various Latin books that he thought would be of use to his people (§ 13). Under his son and grandsons all England south of the Humber gradually became subject to the West-Saxon king; and the Scandinavian element was pretty well absorbed by the English. But some two hundred years after the first "Danes" had come to England, new swarms crossed over (984) from Norway and Denmark and conquered the island, which was now for some time ruled by **Danish kings**. In the next century England was again conquered (1066) by men of Teutonic blood, — the **Normans** (or Northmen), who had been settled now more than a hundred years in France, where they had adopted the French language and the Christian religion.

Language and Literature.*

6. The TEUTONIC or GERMANIC languages are: (1) **Gothic**, (2) **Scandinavian** (including Norwegian and Icelandic, Swedish and Danish), (3) **West Germanic.** The WG. languages are (1) *Low German* (the languages native to the northern lowlands: Plattdeutsch, Dutch, Frisian, English), (2) *High German* (the speech of the middle and southern highlands, from which has developed the literary language now spoken in all parts of the country). The **English language** is thus a peculiarly developed Low-German dialect, nearest akin to Frisian, and more like Dutch and Plattdeutsch than like High German.†

7. We have seen (§ 2) that there were *various* LG. tribes that settled in Britain; and as each tribe had come to speak somewhat differently from the others, we have to deal with various OLD ENGLISH DIALECTS, four of which are important: **Kentish, West-Saxon, Mercian,** and **Northumbrian.** The last two are forms of Anglian speech, WS. was the most prominent Saxon dialect, and Kentish represents the speech of the Jutes. Of these, **West Saxon** has the greatest importance; for under the political supremacy of Wessex (§ 5) and the enlightened policy of Ælfred, it became the literary and official language, and in it are written most of the OE. literary monuments that have been preserved to our day (§ 13). It is therefore best to begin the study of OE. with early West Saxon (eWS.) and

---

* The learner is advised to read Dr. Murray's article on the English Language in *Encyclopædia Britannica*, 9th edition, or that in Webster's *International Dictionary*; and the opening chapters of a good English literature, for example, Ten Brink's. For lists of texts, editions, etc., cf. the appendix to Cook's translation of Sievers' OE. grammar, or Wülker's *Geschichte der angls. Litteratur.*

† Students of Old English who understand Latin or German will be able to make good use of this knowledge if they familiarize themselves with the general scheme of "Grimm's Law."

to regard this as the standard with which to compare other dialects.

8. We have seen (§ 2) that all the settlers called their language *Englisc*, or English, after the *Engle*, or Angles. They occasionally called themselves *Angelseaxan*, or **Anglo-Saxons** (which means English Saxons as distinguished from the continental Saxons, whom they called *Ealdseaxan*, or Old Saxons, as we in America speak of "Old England"; later the word was misunderstood as meaning a combination of Angles and Saxons); but they never called their language Anglo-Saxon. This was first done by scholars of the sixteenth and seventeenth centuries, to whom Old English seemed more a distinct language than an older stage of their own. We are, therefore, justified in joining those who a score of years ago discarded the term Anglo-Saxon as applied to language, and began to call the oldest known form of our speech "**Old English**"* or "First English." 'The oldest dated Ms. containing OE. words is a charter of 679, but some of the English inscriptions that were made in Runic letters (§ 14) are probably older' (Sweet, H.E.S. § 345).

9. The chief periods of English are called **Old, Middle**, and **Modern**. The change from one to the other was, of course, gradual: the transition from OE. to ME. was in the twelfth century; that from ME. to M^{n}E., in the fifteenth. Sweet has well defined OE. as the period of FULL endings (*mōna, sunne, sunu, hringas*); ME. as the period of LEVELLED endings, weak vowels being reduced to a uniform *e* like German final *ę* (*mōne, sunne, sune, ringes*); M^{n}E. as the period of LOST endings (*moon, sun, son, rings*).

10. But it was not always the same dialect that was the **literary language**. We have seen that literature first flourished among the Angles (§ 2), where it was brought to an

---

* "Old English" is still used by some to designate Middle English or early Modern English; so in Webster's and Stormonth's dictionaries.

untimely end by the Danish inroads,* that later WS. became the literary and official language (§ 7), only to be crowded into obscurity when the Normans brought in French (§ 5, end). When English again got the upper hand, it was the dialect of London that became the standard. This was originally a Saxon Dialect, early affected by the neighboring Kentish and Mercian. At all times, but particularly after the city had been depopulated by the great plagues, from various parts of the island people thronged to the capital; as the larger part of the island was Anglian, the dialect of the metropolis gradually assumed a more Anglian, or Mercian (§ 7), character. It was the London dialect in which Chaucer wrote, and from which the modern standard speech is descended.

11. English has been much and often subjected to **external influences**.

a) Even before the emigration from the continent, **Latin** words were learned from the Roman traders that visited the German tribes, from the Germans that served in the armies of the Empire, and in other ways. Thus Lat. *vīnum* > OE. *wīn* M^{n}E. *wine,* Ger. 𝔚ein, similarly with *butter, cheese,* etc.; (*via*) *strāta* > OE. *strǣt* M^{n}E. *street,* 𝔖traße, so with *mile, pound, inch,* etc.; and even the Christian *ęngel,* 𝔈ngel, and *dēofol* M^{n}E. *devil,* 𝔗eufel. Lat. *buxum,* popular Lat. *bucso,* "writing-tablet of box-wood" (used particularly for documents), was associated by the Germans with G^c *bōco-, bōc(j)ōn-* "beech-tree," and > G^c *bōc-s* (OE. OS. *bōc,* OHG. *buoh*) "writing-tablet, charter, book."

b) On the island the conquerors heard both **Latin** and **Celtic**, the former particularly in the towns,† and thus added to their vocabulary (1) many such words as *munt* "mount" < Lat. *montem, pihten* "part of a loom" < Lat. *pecten, bepǣċan* "be-

---

* Even the literary products of the period would have been lost had they not come down to us in copies made by Saxon scribes.

† Cf. Pogatscher: "Zur Lautlehre der gr., lat. und rom. Lehnworte im AE." especially pp. 1–15.

guile, cheat" < Lat. *pāco* "soothe, pacify"; cf. also the proper names *Chester, Wor-cester, Lan-caster*, etc., < OE. *ċeaster* "fortified town" < Lat. *castra*; and (2) such Celtic words as *cradle, mattock, rock, curse*, and many proper names: for example, those, like London, in *don* < Celtic *dūn*, for which the real English word is *tūn* "town." Some of these words the Celts themselves had learned from their Roman conquerors; thus, "ass" < OE. *assa* < Celtic *assan* < Lat. *asinus*, which had long before passed directly into G^c as *asilus*, OE. *ęsol*, Ger. Ejel.

. c) With the introduction of Christianity many **Latin** and **Greek** ecclesiastical terms became popular (thus, *prēost* "priest," *nunne* "nun," *scōl* "school," *nōn* "noon," etc.); and, all along, our language has drawn learned and technical terms from Latin and Greek.

d) Much greater was the influence of the large **Scandinavian** element (§ 5), and to this source we owe many of our most familiar words. Thus, even in OE. we find *tacan* "take" < Sc. *taka* (for which the real English word was *niman* nehmen), *wrang* "wrong," *lagu* "law," and many others. But most of the Sc. words do not appear till later, in the ME. period, when the Sc. population and speech had been absorbed by the English. Words beginning with the sound *sk* are foreign words, and most of them are of Sc. origin, the native E. word having *sh-* < OE. *sċ-*, § 85, 3. Thus *skin, skill, sky, scabby* (the real E. form being *shabby*), *skirt* (for E. *shirt*, both words, like Ger. Schurz and our *short*, being from Late Lat. *ex-curtus*).

e) Still greater was the influence of Norman French (§ 5, end) upon English; but all this happened after the OE. period.

12. We have seen (§ 2) that LITERATURE was first cultivated among the **Angles** of the North. This was toward the close of the seventh century, when Christianity had become established in the country (§ 4), and the new faith was cherished with a rare ardor and devotion. We know that, long before, all Teutonic peoples had been fond of music and song, and that poems, celebrating in sturdy rhythm the deeds of chieftain or god and the glory of war, were composed and recited by travelling minstrels in the hall of the chief, where he and his Gesīths sat drinking mead. Such a poem was the great epic **Bēowulf** (*bay'owulf*). But this, like most of the little of heathen literature that escaped the mistaken zeal of early Christianity, bears traces of Christian conception and faith. Directly inspired by the religion of Jew and Christian was the paraphrase of the Bible composed by **Cædmon** (*kăd'moṇ*) under the patronage of Hilda, Abbess of Whitby. In this as well as in the noble Christian poems of **Cynewulf** (*kü'newulf*), but less in the *Judith*, there reappears the old English delight in the clash of arms and in the struggle with the sea. Lyric poetry prospered less than epic; but there have been a few lyrics (*Dēor's Complaint, The Complaint of the Woman, The Seafarer, The Wanderer*) preserved to us, which generally voice the complaint of one who has suffered, or is lonely. Even in Christian days war-songs were composed that had much of the old poetic fire. Two that celebrate events of the tenth century deserve special mention, *The Battle of Maldon* and *The Battle of Brunnanburh*.

13. PROSE, too, may be said to have begun in the days of Northumbrian culture, for it was at Jarrow that the learned **Bēda** (modern *Bede*), whose Latin writings were the well of scientific and historical knowledge for generations after, translated a part of the Bible into English. But it was particularly during the days of the WS. renaissance (§§ 5, 7) that English prose (eWS., § 7) was much cultivated. We have seen that **King Ælfred** not only encouraged schools and scholarship, but himself translated various Latin books: Boë'thius' *Consolation of Philosophy*, Orosius' *History of the World*, Gregory's *Pastoral Care*, etc. In his day, too, the laws were revised, and the **English** or **Anglo-Saxon Chronicle** became more than a mere list

of events. Later on there was another revival of English prose (late WS.). This time it is the Homilies of the abbot **Ælfric** (written about the year 1000) and of Archbishop **Wulfstān** that attract most attention. Ælfric also translated parts of the Bible, and wrote a Latin grammar in English. He, as well as the WS. monk **Byrhtferth**, who taught in a school at Ramsey on the Isle of Man, revived in English the learning of Bēda.

I. PHONOLOGY.

CHAPTER I.

The Alphabet.

14. The German settlers brought with them an alphabet that was in use among their kinsmen the Goths and Scandinavians as well as among themselves. This was the **Runic Futhark**, a G^c modification of the Latin alphabet, made about 200 A.D. The modification consisted principally in the use of

ᚠ	F *feoh*	ᚺ	H *hægel*	↑	T *tīr*	ᚨ	A *āc*
ᚢ	U *ūr*	ᚾ	N *nied*	ᛒ	B *beorc*	ᚩ	O *ōs*
ᚦ	Þ *þorn*	ᛁ	I *īs*	ᛗ	E *eoh*	ᚣ	Y *ȳr*
ᚫ	{ (A **ans*) / Æ *æsċ* }	ᛃ	(J *ġēar*)	ᛉ	M *męn*	ᛇ	EO *eor*
ᚱ	R *rād*	ᛇ	? *ēoh*	ᛚ	L *lagu*	ᛠ	EA *ear*
ᚳ	Ċ *ċēn*	ᛈ	P *peorð*	ᛝ	N=η *ing*	ᛣ	C *cweorð*
ᚷ	Ġ *ġiefu*	ᛦ	{ (Z) X ? / *eolhseċġ* }	ᛟ	{ (O *ōðil*) / Œ E *ēðel* }	ᚸ	G *gār*
ᚹ	W { *wyn* / *wēn* }	ᛋ	S *siġel*	ᛞ	D *dæġ*	ᛥ	ST *stān*

Obsolete values etc. are in ( ).

perpendicular or oblique lines for horizontal ones, and of angles for curves, and was due to the fact that the runes were, probably, first cut on twigs, which were sometimes used for purposes of divination. There were 24 G⁰ runes, but the changes in OE. utterance caused some changes in the alphabet and the addition of several new characters. As **a** often > **æ** (§ 25, 1) or **o** (§ 25, 4), and as **o** was mutated (§ 43) to **œ** later **e**, and **u** to **y**, new runes were made for **a** and **o** by modifying the old **a**-rune, and one for **y** by changing that for **u**. As a distinction arose between ċ ġ and c g (§§ 55, 56), new runes were made for the latter. When **j** and ġ got the same value (§§ 56 b, 64), the rune of the former was dropped.

NOTE.—After the runes had gone out of general use, they were still occasionally employed in inscriptions, rebuses, &c., or for their name words.

15. With the introduction of Christianity (§ 4) and Latin learning, the **Latin Alphabet** was introduced afresh, and that in the form it had assumed in Ireland, for the Scots of Ireland had more or less to do with the spreading of Christianity among the English. In England the alphabet went its own way. For the **u** or **uu** and the **th** at first employed, the runes ᚹ and ᚦ came into use, and for ᚦ a crossed **d**, that is Ð ð, was often substituted, especially medially and finally.

NOTE 1.—The usual mediæval contractions are not wanting in OE. MSS. Thus ᷄ or ~ over a vowel = **m** (but ðoñ hwoñ = ðonne hwonne), and over a cons. it = **er**, less often **or**. ꝑ (a crossed ꝑ) is the usual way of writing þæt; ond, or and, is rare, being written ⁊ (like &, a contraction of Lat. *et*); and ɫ (a crossed *l* = Lat. *vel*) is often used instead of oððe.

NOTE 2.—Over long vowels (especially if the word is very short) a mark like ´ is often found in MSS.; much less frequently is ˘ found over short vowels. In this book all long vowels are marked with a macron (ā &c.), while short ones are left unmarked.

NOTE 3.—In the earlier editions of OE. texts, types were employed that imitated the letters of the MSS. (so ſ ᴄ ε ᴅ ꝼ ᵹ ᴘ ꞃ ꞅ = S C E d f g r s t), cf. March's *Anglo-Saxon Grammar*; but now ordinary letters are used, only þ or ð, and sometimes ᵹ = g, being retained. For p a **w** (less often **v**) is used.

NOTE 4.—The punctuation of the MSS. is very imperfect; that in printed texts is supplied by the editors.

CHAPTER II.

Speech Sounds and Names.

16. 1) The vibration of the vocal chords produces a sound that is technically called **Voice**. The vowels are all "*voiced*"; consonants may be (for ex. *b, l, w,* &c.), or they may be "*voiceless*" (for ex. *p, h,* &c.).

2) In a **Vowel**, the "voice" is the chief thing, and the modification of the sound (by the varying shape of the vocal passage in the various vowels) is a subordinate matter; in a **Consonant**, voice is secondary and may be entirely wanting, while the local sound (as that at the teeth in the case of *s*, at the lips in the case of *p* or *b*) is the main thing. But some cons⁸ approach very nearly to vowels, for ex. the "semi-vowels" *w* and *j* (= Eng. *y*) are really only unsyllabic (cf. 3) *u* and *i* (= $M^r E$. *oo* and *ee*). So too the "sonorous consonants" (cf. 3) are "vowel-like." The transition sound produced in passing from one sound to another, is called a **Glide** (§§ 55, 56), but glides are not generally noticed.

3) The more **sonorous** a sound, the more likely it is to become syllabic; thus in a diphthong, the more sonorous vl. is syllabic, the other not. Vl⁸ are more sonorous than cons⁸. Of the latter, *l m n r* are pre-eminently "Sonorous Consonants" (§ 20, 1), and hence often syllabic: nægl *nail*, hræfn *raven*.

17. 1) If the tongue is pressed forward during the formation of a vowel, it is called a **Front Vowel** (OE. æ, e, i, &c.); if drawn back, a **Back Vowel** (OE. a, ǫ, o, u).

2) A vowel is said to be **Low, Mid,** or **High**, according as the tongue is lowered a good deal, but moderately, or very little.

3) If the lips are brought close together while a vl. is being sounded, it is called a **Rounded Vowel**. OE. *o* and *œ*

(= Ger. ö) were alike in that both were rounded. while e was not; but œ and e were alike in being front vlⁱ.

4) If a vl. is quickly sounded, it is called "**short**"; if it is prolonged, it is called "**long.**" Cf. § 19, 2.

18.

	back	front		back	front
Simple Vowels { high	—	i	Rounded Vowels { high	u	y
mid	a	e	mid	o	œ
low	—	æ	low	—	—

19. 1) A syllable that ends in a vowel is called an **Open Syllable**; one that ends in a cons., a **Closed Syllable**. A single cons. belongs to the following syllable. Open syllables: *pū, pe, slœ-pe, beo-re*; closed syllables: *blōd, glœd, brin-gan, lib-ban*.

2) A **syllable is long** if it contains a long vowel or diphthong, or if its vowel is followed by more than one cons.

Thus the first syllable is *long* in: blōd, cræft, ðū, slǣpan, cēosan; and *short* in: þe, glæd, hwatu, beore. A long syllable must not be confounded with a long vowel (§ 17, 4).

3) A syllable that is not strongly stressed is called a **Weak Syllable**; its vowel is often different from that in the corresponding **Strong Syllable**. Strong MⁿE. 'my' is sounded *mai*, while weak 'my' is *mă* or *mĭ*. Cf. §§ 48–50, 25, 3, 30 N, 47, 93, 95, 2.

20. 1) A cons. produced by stopping and then exploding the breath, is called a **Shut Consonant** or a **Stop** (also a "Mute"), so *p, t, d*. A cons. produced by allowing the breath to escape through an opening, is called an **Open Consonant**: if the opening is very narrow so that there is much friction of the breath against the walls of the passage, the cons. is called a **Fricative** (or a "Spirant"), thus OE. *s, f, h*; if the opening is not so narrow as to cause marked friction, the cons. is called a **Sonorous Consonant** (§ 16, 3) or a **Semi-Vowel** (§ 16, 2).

2) Cons⁸ made (1) with the lips are called **Lip Consonants** (also "Labials"), so *b, m*, &c.; (2) by the front of the tongue, **Front Consonants** (namely, Point Consˢ, or "Dentals," and Top Consˢ, or "Palatals"), so *t, s, n* and *ċ, ġ*, &c.; (3) by the back of the tongue, **Back Consonants** (also "Gutturals"), *c, h*, &c., § 85.

CHAPTER III.

The WS. Vowels, Their Pronunciation and Source.

1. Simple Vowels.

21.

a is sounded as in MⁿE. *artistic*: dagas "days." [< Gᶜ a § 25,2]
ā as in *art*: stān "stone." [< Gᶜ al § 35,1; WG. ā]ʷ ᵏᶜ· § 30,2,3]
æ " " *mankind*: dæġ "day." [< Gᶜ a § 25,1]
ǣ " " *man*¹: þǣr "there." [<WG. ā § 30,1; ā)¹ § 43,1; æġ]ᵈ· ⁿ § 88]
e, ę " " *men*: stefn, męn. [e < Gᶜ e § 26,1; ę < a)¹ § 43,1, and o)¹ § 43,2]
ē " " *they*²: gēs. [<Gᶜ ē § 31; weak Gᶜ ǣ § 30,1 N; ō)¹ § 43,2; eġ]ᵈ· ⁿ § 88]
i " " *in*: bite "bite." [< Gᶜ i § 27,1; Gᶜ e]ⁿᵃˢ· § 26,2; cf. also § 22 N⁴]
ī " " *machine*: mīn. [<Gᶜī §32,1; 1+nas.]ˢ ᵏᶜ·§72; iġ]ᵈ·ⁿ§88; cf. also 22 N⁴]
o " " N.E. *stone* or Ger. Gott: god. [< Gᶜ o § 28,1; Gᶜ u § 29,2]
ǫ " " *on*: mǫn "man." [< Gᶜ a § 25,4]
ō " " *stone*³: gōd. [< Gᶜ ō §33; Gᶜ ǣ]ⁿᵃˢ· §30,4; ǫ + nas.]ˢ ᵏᶜ· § 72 & N¹]
u " " *full*: wulf. [< Gᶜ u § 29,1; Gᶜ o]ⁿᵃˢ· ᵏᶜ· § 28,2,3; ʷ[1o § 39,1]
ū " " *rule*: hūs "house." [< Gᶜ ū § 34; u + nas.]ˢ ᵏᶜ· § 72]
y " " Ger. Müller⁴: wyllen "woolen." [<u)¹ § 43,3; cf. also § 22 N⁴]
ȳ " " " grün⁴: brȳd "bride." [< ū)¹ § 43,3; yn]ˢ ᵏᶜ· § 72; yġ]ᵈ· ⁿ § 88; cf. also § 22 N⁴]

For œ cf. § 43,2, ft. nt. 2.

---

¹ When prolonged, as is usual in America.

² MⁿE. *ey* in *they*, like "long *a*" in *date* &c., is often a diphthong ending in *ĭ*, while OE. *ē* is the same vowel from beginning to end.

³ In strictness, not the same; for MⁿE. "long *o*" is often a diphthong ending in *ŭ*, while OE. *ō* is a pure vowel.

⁴ Ger. grün and Müller are like E. *green* and *miller*, but the lips are nearly closed — or "rounded" — during the formation of the vowel.

2. Diphthongs.

22. Note 1. — In the OE. diphthong the first element (whether long or short) is syllabic (§ 16, 3), or has the stress; but in some cases the stress shifted later to the second element. For *ġeāra* cf. § 40 N[1].

Note 2. — *ēa* and *ēo* are from older *au* and *eu* and their second element (whether written *a* or *o*) was an obscure unaccented vowel, a reduction of *u*. The *a* of *au* became *æ* (cf. § 25, 1(2)), and *ea* would better be written *æa*, as it sometimes was; but the *e* of *eo* is a true *e*.

ea $= æ' + a^1$: heard. [$< æ$] § 41; $a)^u$ § 44; pal.[$æ$ § 40]
ēa $= \bar{æ}' + a^1$: hēafod. [$<$ G^c au § 36; $a + o$ or u § 45; pal.[$\bar{æ}$ § 40]
eo $= e' + o$: eorðe. [$< e$] and i] § 41; $e)^{u, o}$ and $i)^{u, o}$ § 44; pal.[o or u § 40]
ēo $= \bar{e}' + o$: cēosan. [$<$ G^c eu § 37; pal. [$\bar{o}$ § 40; e or $i +$ back vl. § 45]
ie $= i' + e$: ieldra. [$<$ ea)^1 or eo)^1 § 43, 4, 5; eo]pal, § 40, 2); $i)^{u, o}$ § 44]
īe $= \bar{i}' + e$: hīeran. [$<$ ēa)^i or ēo)^i § 43, 4, 5]

Note 3. — *eo* and *io* sometimes had different origins, but even in eWS. they were confounded, and *eo* supplanted *io*.

Note 4. — *ie* and *īe* were often written *i*, later *y*: from which Lloyd infers that *ie* assumed a sound intermediate to *i* and *e*; while *y*, on becoming unrounded (§ 17, 3), was reduced to the same sound.

For weak vowels cf. §§ 48–50.

---

[1] *æ'a* with prefixed *y* may be heard in the colloquial *yæah* = "yes," and *ǣ'a* in the same word when drawled.

CHAPTER IV.

I. The G^c and the WG. Vowel System.

23. Primitive Germanic had the following: —
Short vowels: a   e   i   o   u
Long vowels: ā   ǣ & ē   ī   ō   ū
Diphthongs: ai
                au   eu

NOTE 1. — Some of the *i*'s were once *e*'s; for Indo-European $e > G^c\ i$: —
1) before nas.+cons. (cf. Lat. offendimentum with OE. **bindan**);
2) when *i* or *j* stood in the next syllable (so inf. *helpan* but 3 s. ind. *hilpð* (< orig. *hilpið*) § 43 N². (Perhaps this happened in WG. times.)
So, too, $ei > ii > \bar{\imath}$ as in Latin (Gr. δείκνυμι, Lat. *dīcō*, G^c *tīhan*, OE. *tēon*, § 46, 1 (3)).

NOTE 2. — Some *o*'s were once *u*'s; for older $u > o$ if the next slb. had *a* (or *o*, N³), unless this was prevented by intervening nas.+cons., or *i, j* (by which the *u* was later mutated to *y* § 43, 3). Thus we have G^c **giholpan** (OE. ġeholpen) but **gibundan** (OE. ġebunden) and **huggian** (OE. hyċġan).

NOTE 3. — IE. $o > G^c\ a$ (Lat. octo, Goth. **ahtau**, OE. **eahta**, § 41, *eight*), but the unstressed *o* of endings remained *o* longer, in certain positions probably into primitive OE. times, § 49, 1.

24. The WG. system differed from the G^c only in having *ā* for older *ǣ* § 30, 1.

II. What the G^c Vowels became in WS. §§ 25–50.

A. *Chiefly of Stem Vowels.* §§ 25–47.

1. General Changes. §§ 25–37.

a) *Short Vowels.* §§ 25–29.

25. 1) $a > æ$ (1) in closed (§ 19, 1) slb^r: **dæġ** *day*.
    $æ] > ea$ § 41, and $ea)^1 > ie$ § 43, 4.
    $æġ]^{d, n} > \bar{æ}$ § 88.

(2) sometimes in open slb⁸ if next slb. has e: dæ-ġes day's; and in ēa < au § 22 N².
(3) if next slb. had i or j, but œ)¹ > e § 43, 1. Cf. 2) end.
2) **a** remains a in open slb⁸ if next slb. has a, o, or u (or a vl. derived from one of these): da-gas, da-gum, days; macīan (ī < ōj) make.
a)ᵘ > ea § 44.
3) **a** in weak slb⁸ (§ 19, 3): —
   (1) remains **a**: ac but,   herepað } but pæð.
   (2) > **o**: of of Ger. ab, herepoð }
   So pone &c., and weak on but strong ǫn (stressed adv.); weak ot was displaced by strong æt.
4) a]ⁿᵃˢ· > ǫ § 38, 1 (1), ǫ)ⁱ > ę § 43, 1; ǫ + nas.]ˢ ᵏᶜ· > ō § 72, ō)ⁱ > ē § 43, 2].
5) a + o or u > ēa § 45.
For ᵖᵃˡ·⌈a, or rather œ, cf. § 40.

26. 1) **e** often remains **e**: beran bear.
2) e]ⁿᵃˢ· > i § 38, 2).
3) e⌉ > eo § 41, eo)ⁱ > ie § 43, 5 } ʷ⌈eo > o § 39, 2.
4) e)ᵘ > eo § 44   }
5) eġ]ᵈ·ⁿ > ē § 88.
6) e + back vl. > ēo § 45.
For ᵖᵃˡ·⌈e cf. § 40.

27. 1) **i** often remains **i**: witan know.
2) i⌉ > io § 41, io)ⁱ > ie § 43, 5 } ʷ⌈io > u § 39, 1.
3) i)ᵘ > io § 44   }
4) in]ˢ ᵏᶜ· (§ 72) and iġ]ᵈ·ⁿ (§ 88) > ī.
5) i + back vl. > īo or ēo § 45.
i + e > īe § 45.

28. 1) **o** generally remains **o**: god god, folc, word.
2) **o**, espec. next labials, often > **u**: wulf, lufu.
3) o]ⁿᵃˢ· > u § 38, 3, u)ⁱ > y § 43, 3.
4) o)ⁱ > e § 43, 2.

NOTE. — When (so espec. in foreign words) o was followed by i, and analogy did not prevent (§ 43, 2, ft. nt. 3 end), o > u and u)ⁱ > y: Scottas Scyttisc, box byxen. Cf. Pogatscher §§ 223 ff.

29. 1) u often remains u: hund *dog*.
2) u > o in *or-*: ordāl Ger. Urteil *judgment*.
3) un]¹ &c. > ū § 72; ū)ⁱ > ȳ § 43, 3.
For ᵖᵃˡ·⌈u > eo cf. § 40.

b) *Long Vowels.* §§ 30–34.

30. I. WG. ā (< Gᶜ ǣ): —
1) ā generally > ǣ: æfen Abend *evening*.

NOTE. — Weak (§ 19, 3) ǣ > ē: Ælfrēd, hīrēd Heirat.

2) ā]ʷ remains ā: tāwīan *prepare*, ā)ⁱ > ǣ § 43, 1: æltǣwe *complete*, cf. § 43, N¹.
3) ā]ᵇᵃᶜᵏ ᵛˡ· > ă or ǣ (cf. § 40 N¹): lāgon lǣgon, lācnīan lǣcnīan *heal*, and)ⁱ > ǣ: lǣċe *physician*.
4) ā]ⁿᵃˢ· > ō § 38, 1 (3), ō)ⁱ > ē § 43, 2.
5) ā]ʰ⁺ᶜᵒⁿˢ· > ă > ea, and *eah* may > ēa: smēaliċ *dainty*, cf. § 91 & 2.

For ᵖᵃˡ·⌈ǣ cf. § 40.

II. Gᶜ and WG. nasalized ā (< an]ʰ) > ō § 72 N¹, ō)ⁱ > ē § 43, 2.

31. ē remains ē: hēr *here*.

32. 1) ī generally remains ī: mīn *mine*, wīf *wife*.
2) ī]ʰ⁺ᶜᵒⁿˢ· > ĭ (§ 46 II.) and then (§ 41, 3) eo: leoht, Ger. leicht *light*, so *betwīhnum > betweohnum (§ 91, & 2) > betwēonum *between*.
3) ī + back vl. > īo, ēo § 45, 1 (3).

33. 1) ō generally remains ō: gōd *good*, ō)ⁱ > ē § 43, 2.
2) Final stressed ō > ū: cū *cow*, tū *two*; but weak tō.

34. ū remains ū: tūn *town*, ū)ⁱ > ȳ § 43, 3.

c) *Diphthongs.*

35. 1) ai > ā: stān Stein *stone*, ā)ⁱ > ǣ § 43, 1.
2) ai]ʷ > ā rarely ō: snāw *snow*, ā or ō (< aiw) *ever*.

36. au > ēa (§ 22 and N¹·²): ēac auch *eek*, ēa)ⁱ > īe § 43, 4.

37. eu > ēo (§ 22 and N¹·²): dēop *deep*, ēo)ⁱ > īe § 43, 5.

2. Chief Effects of Neighboring Sounds upon Stem Vowels. §§ 38–46.

a) *Influence of Nasals* (⸣ⁿᵃˢ·).

38. 1) G^c *a* acquired before nasals a sound like that of *o* in *on*, or of *a* in *ball*; as there was no letter to represent the new sound, it was in the MSS. sometimes spelled *a*, and sometimes *o*. Sweet first suggested the use of ǫ for this "open *o*."

(1) a⸣ⁿᵃˢ· > ǫ : mǫn, lǫnd, cǫmb, lǫng.
    on⸣ᵃᵖⁱʳᵃⁿᵗ > ō § 72 : gōs < gǫns Ganŝ *goose*.
(2) Nasalized G^c ā⸣ʰ > OE. ō § 72 N : þōhte dachte *thought*. Cf. § 46 II.
(3) G^c ǣ, WG. ā⸣ⁿᵃˢ· also > ō § 30, 4 : ġedōn gethan *done*.

2) e⸣ⁿᵃˢ· > i : niman nehmen *take*. Cf. § 24 N¹.
3) o⸣ⁿᵃˢ· > u : ðunor Donner *thunder*.

b) *Influence of* w (ʷ⸢ *and* ⸣ʷ).

39. 1) ʷ⸢*io* (< *i* § 27, 2, 3) usually > *u* : wuduwe, (less often) weoduwe, or widuwe *widow*.

2) ʷ⸢*eo* (< *e* § 26, 3, 4) sometimes > *o* : worold, (more usually) weorold Welt *world*.

3) *a*⸣ʷ and *e*⸣ʷ > *au* and *eu*, and these (§§ 36, 37) > *ēa* and *ēo* : fēawe *few*, þēowas *servants*.

4) *i*⸣ʷ > *iu* > *io*, but *īo*)¹ > *īe* : nīewe *new*.
    Cf. also § 28, 2.

c) *Influence of Palatals* (ᵖᵃˡ·⸢ *and* ⸣ᵖᵃˡ·).

40. 1) Influence of Initial Palatal.

(a) For older *jæ*, *jo*, we usually find *gea*, *geo* (Ger. Jahr OE. gēar *year*, Joch geoc *yoke*) and *ju* is spelled both *iu* and *geo* (iung, geong *young*).

(b) So after the palatals (ġ, ċ, sċ) we find not *œ*, *ǣ*, *e*, but *ea*, *ēa*, *ie* : geaf (for gæf), gēafon (for gǣfon) *gave*, giefan (for gefan) *give*, ceaf (for cæf) *chaff*, sceal (for scæl) *shall*.

NOTE 1. — This spelling is differently interpreted by OE. scholars. In general we shall follow Sievers and Sweet, who are substantially agreed that the palatal cons. was succeeded by a glide (§ 16, 2) which with the following vl. formed a diphthong, this diphthong coming in time to have the stress on the first element, like other diph⁸ (§ 22). But the gen. pl. *gēura* (MⁿE. *yore*) = *jāra* (§ 30, 3) and has the spelling *ge* instead of *g* by analogy to *gēar* (MⁿE. *year*) < *jǣr* (§ 30, 1); "*gēara*" is therefore to be written *ġeāra*, and "*gēar*" *ġear*.

NOTE 2. — Between the guttural *g* and *c*, and the back, or guttural, vowels *a*, *ǫ*, *o*, *u*, as well as their *i*-mutations, no *i* or *e* occurs: gōd *good*, Cęnt *Kent*.

NOTE 3. — The *e* or *i* sometimes found between *sc* and back vl⁸ (sc(e)acan *shake*, sc(e)ōh *shoe*) is a glide (in eWS. still unstressed), §§ 16, 56, and shows that the *c* had become palatalized by the *s*, the first step toward the modern *sh*, §§ 11 d, 85, 3. This unstressed *e*, *i*, may be printed *ę*, *į*.

2) Influence of Following Palatal (Sievers' "Palatalumlaut"), cf. § 54.

In eWS. this is manifested only in *eo*]ᵖᵃˡ· > *ie*: reoht > rieht *right*. Cf. § 41, 3 (*e* and *i*).

d) *The Breakings* (]).

41. Before certain guttural sounds, the front vl⁸ *e*, *œ*, and *i* acquire a more guttural quality, and are said to be broken into two elements (cf. the pronunciation *wœ'al* for MⁿE. *well*).

1) Before **r** + consonant.
    e > eo : steorra Stern *star*;
    œ (< Gᶜ a) > ea (really *œa* § 22 N²) : earm *arm*;
    i > io, and io)ⁱ > ie : hierde Hirte *herdsman*.

2) Before **l** + consonant.
    œ (< Gᶜ a) generally > ea : feallan *fall*.
    e > eo only before *l* + guttural *c* or *h* : meolcan melken *milk*, eolh *elk*.

3) Before **h** + cons. and before final **h**.
    œ (< Gᶜ a) > ea : eahta acht *eight*.

e > eo : seox ſedȝ̇ *six*, but in most of the words the *h* later > palatal and changed *eo* to **ie**: siex *six* § 40, 2.

i > eo and this (§ 40, 2)) > **ie** : Peohtas, Piehtas *the Picts*.

e) *The Mutations.*

42. Mutation (Ger. Umlaut) is the change produced in a stressed vl. by a following vl. or semi-vowel (§ 20, 1). If the mutating vl. is the high front vl., the vl. before it is assimilated to it (that is, if back, it > front; if already front, it > higher § 17, 2); if the mutating vl. is a back vl., only the latter part of the preceding vl. becomes assimilated, or guttural, and thus a diphthong is produced.

NOTE. — Mutation may affect an intervening unstressed or weakly stressed vl. before reaching the stressed vl. : ā-buri *any time* > *ābyri > *ǣbyri > *ǣberi > ǣbre > ǣfre, *ever*.

(I.) I-*mutation* ( )ⁱ).

43. NOTE 1. — The *i* or *j* that caused)ⁱ appears as *i* only after *r*; elsewhere it sometimes became *e* (§ 48), but it generally disappeared entirely (§ 66 N). The ōj of the II. class of weak verbs > ī too late to cause)ⁱ.

NOTE 2. — The earliest instance of)ⁱ, namely *e > i*, occurred early in G⁰ times, and is not generally classed with the later mutations, cf. § 24 N¹ (2). The)ⁱ of *ǣ*, which is *ǣ*, may be ignored.

1) § 25 a > $\begin{Bmatrix} æ, \text{æ})^i \\ ǫ, ǫ)^i \end{Bmatrix}$ > ę.¹ $\begin{cases} \text{hęrian } praise, \text{ lęċgan } (< \text{lagjan}) \\ \text{lay, męn } men. \end{cases}$

ā)ⁱ > ǣ̃: hǣlan (< hāljan < hāl *whole*) *heal*.

2)² o)ⁱ > ę¹: dohtor, but dat. sg. dęhter,³ *daughter*.

ō)ⁱ > ē: dēman (< dōmjan < dōm *judgment*) *judge*.

3) u)ⁱ > y: hynġran *to hunger* < hungor³ *hunger*.

ū)ⁱ > ȳ: betȳnan (< betūnjan < tūn *enclosure*) *enclose*.

[1] This *e* is well printed ę in grammars and dictionaries, to distinguish it from old *e* § 21. A few words have *œ* for *ę*: fæstan *fasten*, sǣċ *strife*.

[2] o)ⁱ and ō)ⁱ first > œ and ǿ (that is, > front vlˢ, § 17, but retained the rounding of the *o*, § 18), but like other front vlˢ they early lost the rounding and > *e, ē*. Cf. M. and S. Ger. *Getter* for *Götter*. Cf. § 14.

[3] *u* usually > *o* (§ 23 N²), but generally not when *i* or *j* followed; and so when mutation took place, it was *u* that was mutated and consequently

4) ea)¹ > ie : eald *old* but ieldra *older*.
ēa)¹ > īe : hēah *high* but hīehra *higher*.
5) eo)¹ and io)¹ > ie : weorpan *throw* but 3 sg. wierpð (ð<ið).
ēo)¹ and īo)¹ > īe : lēoht *light* but līehtan *to light*.

NOTE. — For *ie* > *i, y* cf. § 22 N⁴.

(II.) **U-** and **O-***mutation* ( )ᵘ,)ᵒ).

44. Cf. § 42. WS. was less affected by this mutation than other dialects; and many forms that once showed it have become levelled under neighboring ones that did not have it. The high vl. *u* (§ 17, 2) was more effective than the mid vl. *o*, which did not affect the mid vl. *a* at all.)ᵘ and)ᵒ seldom operated across a palatal cons. (§ 85, 2) or two or more cons⁸.

NOTE. — The *u* or *o* that caused mutation is not often preserved as such: *u* appears as *u* or *o*; *o* always as *a*; *ō* in almost any form.

1) a)ᵘ > ea : ealu *ale*. (Rare)
   e)ᵘ > eo : heofon *heaven*. (Frequent)
   i)ᵘ > io, eo, ie : lim *limb* pl. leomu, siendun *are*. (")
2) a)ᵒ. (Does not occur, cf. § 44)
   e)ᵒ > eo : ċeole *throat*. (Rare)
   i)ᵒ > io, eo : teolian *to aim*. (Occasional)

f) *Hiatus, Contraction, &c.*

45. Two vl⁸ sometimes (particularly through the dropping out of an *h*, less often *w* or *j*) come to stand next each other, — that is, an hiatus is formed.

I. If the first of the two vl⁸ is unstressed, it becomes silent: be-ūtan > būtan > MⁿE. *but*.

II. If the first vl. is stressed —

1) The two form a diphthong, the second element being an obscure vl. spelled *a, o,* or *e*. (For unstressed *o* see § 23 N³.)

> *y*. (For *o*]¹ > *u* and *u*)¹ > *y* cf. § 28 N.) But as *u* > *o* in most of the forms of such a word as *dohtor*, it did so by analogy in the dat. too, though it was there followed by *i*.

(1) a + o or u > ēa: *sla(h)on > slēan ſchlagen *slay.*
ā (< Gᶜ ǣ) + o or u > ēa: *nā(h)or > nēar *nearer.*
(2) e + back vl. > ēo: *seh(w)on > sēon ſehen *see.*
e + e > ē: *te(h)en > tēn zehn *ten.*
(3) ĭ + back vl. > īo, ēo: *tī(h)on > tēon *censure.*
i + e > īe: *si(j)e > sīe *be.*

2) The second element is usually assimilated to the first and so disappears. (For unstressed o see § 24 N³.)
(1) ō + vl. > ō: *hō(h)on > hōn *hang.*
(2) ū + vl. are not changed or > ū: būan or būn *build.*
(3) ȳ + vl. > ȳ: *fȳir (< *fūir) > fȳr *fire.*
(4) ā (< Gᶜ ai) + vl. > ā: *tai(h)a > tā *toe.*
(5) ēa + vl. > ēa: *hēa(h)es > hēas, gen. sg. of hēah *high.*
(6) ēo + vl. > ēo: *tēo(h)on > tēon *draw.*

3. Changes in Quantity.

46. The quantities usually assigned to the OE. vlˢ are what may be called historic quantities. That is, such changes in quantity as have taken place in OE. as distinguished from WG., are usually ignored. The reason for this is that it is very difficult to determine just when and where the changes took place.

(I.) *Lengthening.*

1) It is certain that final stressed vowels > long: þū *thou,* hwā *who,* sē *he* or *that*; but unstressed sĕ *the,* hĕ, the rel. þĕ, &c., similarly eal-swā *just so,* Mⁿ *also,* but weak (§ 93, 2) ealswa *as.*

2) There was a tendency to lengthen vlˢ before a sonant cons. + a voiced stop (§ 20, 1: bīndan, wōrd, gōld, cǭmb), but this seems not to have been true of all vlˢ, nor universally the case before *nd* and *ng*. These lengthenings will not be noticed in this book.

(II.) *Shortening.*

A vl. before h + cons. > short: þōhte > þohte, *wīh-bēod > *wihbeod > *weohbod (§ 32, 2; for ēo > eo > o in bēod, cf. § 48 end) > wēofod (§ 91 & 2, § 76 N¹) *altar.*

4. Vowel Gradation.

47. 1) Gradation (Ger. Ablaut) is a difference of vowel due to a difference of accent (cf. § 19, 3) in Indo-European times in various forms of a word or in related words.

With Greek ϝεῖδον, ϝοῖδα, ϝιδεῖν or Lat. vidēre, vīsus, compare OE. *wītan (ī<ei, § 23 N¹ end), wāt (ā<ai, § 35, <oi, § 23 N³), witon, wīs.

The difference of accent can no longer be seen, for in G⁰ times the stress came to be uniformly placed upon the first slb. of simple words (§ 94), and some of the older accented slb' fell away, § 50.

2) Gradation plays in G⁰ its chief role in the verb, which shows six gradation series: —

1	ī (<ei̯ § 24 N²)	ai̯	i	i
2	eu̯	au̯	u	u (o)
3	e (i)	a	u	u (o)
4	e (i)	a	ǣ	u (o)
5	e (i)	a	ǣ	e
6	a	ō	ō	a

1–5 have the gradation e/o (G⁰ e/a, § 23 N⁸, or i/a, § 23 N¹), with the changes due to the following cons. (1 and 2, the semi-vowels j and w, or $i̯, u̯$; 3, sonorous cons. + cons.; 4, simple sonorous cons.; 5, nonsonorous cons.); 6 has the gradation $a/ā$ (G⁰ $a/ō$).

Gradation continues in OE., but, in consequence of the many changes in the various vl' (§§ 25 ff.), the subject appears more complicated, §§ 00 ff.

B. *The Vowels of Medial and Final Syllables.*

a) *Quantity and Quality.*

48. The vowels in unstressed slb' are all short, but e and i long kept their length under a slight accent in the endings *-ēre* (leornēre *learner*, § 97 b) and *-ian* of the II. weak conjugation. Old œ and i generally $> e$: $ārœ > āre$ g. d. a. sg. & n.

a. pl. of ār *honor*; rīċi (§ 49 N¹) > rīċe *realm*, hilpis > hilpes(t) *helpest*; but a slight stress generally preserved *i* in the derivative endings *-iġ, -ing, -isċ,* cf. also § 43 N¹. For *i* + vl. : *j* + vl. cf. § 66 N. An *u* is often lowered to *o*, *o* unrounded to *a*, and this fronted to *e*. The vowel in a syllable that once had at least secondary stress but has lost it, is apt to become short and to be reduced to an obscure vowel usually written *e* or *o*; so *mis'līċ'* > *mis'liċ,* and *mis'licor* > *mis'lecor*; *hlāf'w(e)ard'* > *hlā'ford*, § 25, 3. Cf. also § 19, 3, and 95, 2.

b) *Gradation* (cf. § 47).

49. I. ANCIENT GRADATION. The IE. gradation series *e/o* appears in G⁰ as *i/o* or *a*, and (though all these vlˢ may have > *e*) the gradation can still be recognized in OE. in such forms as ǣgen/āgen *own,* the first only showing)¹, § 43.

II. RECENT GRADATION. Unstressed *o* and *u* > *e* if the next slb. contains a back vl., and similarly *ung* > *ing*: rodor rodores/roderas *heaven*; sealfode/sealfedon *anointed*; leornung/leorninga *learning.* But cf. §

c) *Apheresis, Syncope, Apocope* (cf. also § 45, I., II.).

50. NOTE 1. — The loss of a sound is termed apheresis, syncope, or apocope, according as it is initial, medial, or final.

NOTE 2. — Before disappearing, a vl. generally > the "mid-mixed," or "obscure," vl., usually written *e*; hence vlˢ that are already mid disappear sooner than high vlˢ. Cf. § 17.

1) Apheresis is rare in native words (ræfnan < ar-æfnan *perform*), but it frequently happened to foreign words adopted into G⁰ speech: episcopus > bisċop *bishop,* epistula > pistol *letter.*

2) Syncope occurs according to the following important rule: —

After a long slb. (§ 19, 2) an originally short medial vl. is dropped unless it be guarded by more than one cons.: dēofol

VOWEL GRADATION — WEAK SYLLABLES. 27

dēofles < *dēofoles; but rodor rodores, as rod- is a short slb.; and roccettan, as e is guarded by the two cons' tt.

NOTE 1. — Trisyllabic f. and nt. forms in -u do not syncopate: īdelu *idle*, nīetenu *cattle* (but fem' in -(i)ðu syncopate regularly: stręngðu *strength*); on the other hand, micel *large* regularly and yfel *evil* generally syncopate in spite of the shortness of the stem vl.: micles, yfles.

NOTE 2. — Analogy sometimes levels the forms that arise from this law; thus we find dēofoles (for dēofles) by analogy to dēofol, and adjectives with short stems, like hwæt, have (not -ere -ene, but) -re -ne, just as gōd has gōdre gōdne.

NOTE 3. — The e of the 2d and 3d pers. sg. ending (-es(t) -eð) of strong verbs and of weak verbs of the I. class is generally dropped in WS.

3) Apocope.

I.) The original final mid vl' *a, o,* and *e,* fall away (§ 50 N²): Greek ἀνά, G° ana, OE. on; *dōmoz (§ 24 N³) > *dōmo (§ 68 N) > dōm *judgment*; voc. dōme > dōm.

II.) The high vl' *i* and *u* regularly fall away only after long slb'(§ 19, 2): *wurmi > wyrm, but wini > wine; wordu > word, while hofu retains *u.* Still *u* is dropped after a short medial slb. that follows a short stem vl.: *firinu > firen *crime*.

NOTE 1. — But the *i* after long slb' (§ 66 N) which became final by the apocope of a following vl. (§ 49, 1), did so too late to be affected by this law. It > *e,* § 48: rīcio- > rīci > rīce *realm*.

NOTE 2. — When, in consequence of apocope, the semi-vowel *w* or a sonorous cons. (§ 20, 1) becomes final, it becomes syllabic (§ 16, 3): barw- > bearu *forest*; æcr *field*, fugl *bird*, tācn *sign*, māðm *treasure*. Before a sonant cons., espec. before *r*, an obscure vl. (generally written *e* after palatal vl', *o* after guttural) is sometimes inserted: æcer, fugol, tācen, māðum.

CHAPTER V.

The Pronunciation of the WS. Consonants. §§ 51–56.

51. p, b, m, w; t, d, r, l have their ordinary MⁿE. values: bewit'an, dyppan, mǣre, lēt. But in making r, the front of the tongue was turned back, and thus r acted like a guttural in "breaking" front vl⁸, § 41. Similarly, OE. l, like MⁿE. l, often had a guttural quality. For k and q cf. § 86, for v § 78, for x § 84.

52. The fricatives f, s, þ (or ð) were —

1) **Voiceless** (or as in MⁿE. for, so, thick, § 16), when *initial* or *final*, but medially only when *doubled* or *next a voiceless cons.*: forð *forth*, scēaf *sheaf*, þæs *of the*; snoffa *snuffles*, scęððan *injure*, cyssan *kiss*; ġepofta *companion*, wascan *wash*;

2) **Voiced** (or as in MⁿE. of, rose, the, § 16), when *between vowels or voiced cons*: ofer *over*, sealfīan *to salve*, furðor *further*, hǣðen *heathen*, ārīsan *arise*.

53. n generally represents MⁿE. dental *n*, as in nōn *noon*; but before dental, palatal, and guttural cons⁸, it too is dental (bindan *bind* and probably in sęnġan (= sendʒan) *singe*, § 55, I. N, end), palatal (Ęnġlisċ *English*), or guttural (Ǫngelcyn *the Angles*); for the two last, a letter like η is sometimes used in grammars.

54. 1) **h** originally stood for the voiceless back open cons. heard in Ger. ach, and it still often had that value (hēah *high*, hliehhan *laugh*); before *t*, and to some extent before *h* and *s*, it palatalized, or became front (so reoht > reoht > rieht, § 40, 2)), or as in Ger. ich.

NOTE. — The back and the front ch-sounds may be learned by whispering respectively *koo* and *key* and dwelling on the sound that follows the *k*.

PRONUNCIATION OF THE WS. CONSONANTS. 29

2) Initially **h** early became the weak glottal cons. heard in M^nE., as in hund *hound*. Initial **hl, hn, hr, hw** were either pronounced as $h + l$, $h + n$, &c. or as voiceless (§ 16) l, n, &c. (hlædder *ladder*, hnutu *nut*, hrōf *roof*, hwǣr *where*); later this *h* generally became silent, but for **hw**, which is now written *wh*, one may hear $h + w$, voiceless w, or voiced w. For *hs* cf. § 90, 4 N.

55. g was —
1) A **shut cons.** (§ 20) I. after *n*,[*] II. when doubled.
   I. After *n* : —

g was sounded as in M^nE. *go* ; þing *thing*, long, cyning *king*.

ġ (§ 85) was articulated farther toward the front of the mouth, like M^nE. *g* in *give* : Ęnġlisċ *English*.

NOTE. — If a vl. followed, a glide intervened (as in the dialectic pronunciation *gyirl* for *girl*), which may have been a remnant of the original *i*, *j* (§ 85, 2); it was sometimes written *e*, but was often not indicated at all : sęnġ(e)an *singe*. It is very probable that this *ġj* had even in OE. times passed through *dj* to *dȝ*, spelled (*d*)*ge* in M^nE., cf. *ġġ* below.

   II. When doubled : —

gg was sounded like *g* in *go*, but was held, or prolonged : dogga *dog*, frogga *frog*.

ġġ was written **cg** and was pronounced like *ġę* in sęnġ(e)an (I. N above), that is, early *ġj*, later *dj* (cf. miċġern *suet* < middġearn) or *dȝ* : hryċġ *back, ridge*, bryċġ *bridge*.

2) An **open cons.** (§ 20) elsewhere.

g was like North Ger. g in Tage (or like M^nE. cons. *y* made far back in the mouth) : gōd *good*, dagas *days*, ġenōg *enough*.

ġ (§ 85) was like M^nE. cons. *y* (cf. also § 88 N) : dæġ *day*, ġēar *year*, nigontiġ *ninety*, ġelīefan *believe*.

56. c was sounded like *c* in *cool* : cuman *come*, cyning *king*, Cęnt *Kent*, cwic *quick*, bucca *buck*. For *cs* cf. § 84 end.

ċ (§ 85) was articulated farther toward the front of the mouth, like *k* in *kill*, but was followed by a glide (as in the

---

[*] Perhaps *g* was a fricative after *n* in eWS. and only > a stop in lWS.

dialectic pronunciation of *sky*, § 16, 2 end), which may have been a remnant of the original *i*, *j* (§ 85, 2); before a back vl. this glide was sometimes written *e* or *i*, but often was not indicated at all: ċild *child*, rīċe *rich*, tǣċ(e)an *teach*, ręċċ(e)an *relate*. It is very probable that this *ċj* had even in OE. times passed through *tj* (ort-ġeard is early written orċeard *orchard*) to *tʃ*, spelled (*t*)*ch* in MⁿE. For *sċ* cf. § 85, 3.

———◆———

CHAPTER VI.

General Matters as to Gᶜ, WG., and OE. Consonants. §§ 57–61.

a) Verner's Law.

57. We sometimes find in an OE. word an **r, d, g,** or **w** where a related word or another form of the same word would lead us to expect **s, ð,** or **h**: —

s — r : { rīsan *rise* ! rǣran *rear*,
{ ċēosan *choose* ! coren *chosen*;

ð — d : { līðan *travel* ! lǣdan *lead*,
{ sēoðan *seethe* ! soden *sodden*;

h — g : { tīen < *tihen *ten* ! twēntiġ *twenty*,
{ slēan < *slahon *slay* ! slæġen *slain*;

h(w) — w : sēon < *seh(w)on *see* ! sāwon *saw*.

Note. — This is what was still manifest in OE. of a Gᶜ law according to which after a slb. not having the primary accent a voiceless fricative > voiced (for ex. *s* > *z*). The full applicability of the law cannot be made plain to beginners: from the first there were exceptions, and later the primitive accent (§ 94 ft. nt.) largely changed, and some of the fricatives underwent modification (for ex., *z* > *r*, and *ð* > *d*, while all voiceless fricatives > voiced between vlˢ, § 52).

b) G^c **ft, ht, ss.**

58. Before **t** we find only the voiceless fricatives **f, h, (þ)**, though a related word or some other form of the same word might lead us to expect a stop or a voiced fricative; and **þt > ss**.

ft : ġiefan (f = v) *give* geben : ġift *gift* Gift.
ht : maġan *can* mögen: meaht *might* Macht.
ss : witan *know* : wisse *knew* and ġewis(s) *certain*.

c) GEMINATION.

59. 1) Any cons. (ex. the semi-vowels *j* and *w*, § 16,2) may occur doubled, but *ġġ* (spelled *ċġ*) became differentiated into *ġj* later *dʒ*, § 55, II).

(a) *G^c Gemination* (mostly due to the assimilation of *n* to a preceding cons.): wulle *wool*, steorra, *star*, mon(n) monnes *man*, swimman *swim*.

(b) *WG. Gemination* (due to *j*: every WG. single cons. ex. r was doubled by a following *j*, provided the cons. was immediately preceded by a short vl.; after long slbs. *j* fell away, § 66): Goth. saljan, OS. selljan, OE. sellan *give*, so hliehhan *laugh*, smiðð e *smithy*, leċġ(e)an *lay*; but Goth. nasjan, OE. nerian (= nerjan) *save*. For voiced *ff* we find the double stop *bb*: hebban *heave*. After long stems: *dōmjan > dēman *deem*, § 66 N.

(c) *OE. Gemination* (due to following *r* or *l*, but not regular): bit(t)or *bitter*, æp(p)el *apple*.

2) *The Simplification of Gemination.* Every gemination (ex. *ċġ*, which was no longer a real geminate, cf. 1 above) was simplified —

(a) When final: eal ealles; mon monnes.

(b) Next another cons.: ealre ealles; cyste cyssan, sende < send-de *sent*.

But etymological spellings (eall &c.) are not uncommon.

PHONOLOGY.

d) ASSIMILATION AND DISSIMILATION.

60. I. *Assimilation.* There is a tendency to make adjacent sounds similar or alike — to make them in the same way or in the same place: *biddeð* 'biddeth' > (§ 50, 2 N³) *biddð* > (§ 59, 2b) *bidð*, but as *ð* was voiceless (§ 52) it made *d* so, that is, changed it to *t*, *bitð*, then *ð* assimilated to *t* and we get *bitt*, which may > *bit* (§ 59, 2a). For *ds* > *ts*, *ts* > *ss*, &c. cf. § 80. For *sr* > *ss* and *lr* > *ll* cf. § 70.

II. *Dissimilation.* a) It seems difficult to sound two fricatives in succession. In OE. one of the two is generally stopped (§ 20), that is, *ð* > *t*, *h* > *c*, &c.: *fifða* 'fifth' > *fifta*, so *siexta*, but *feorða* &c.; *hilpes þu* > *hilpestu* 'helpest thou'; *siehs* > *siecs* or *siex* 'six.' More rarely one fricative was assimilated or lost: *blið s* > *bliss* 'bliss,' *þīhsl* > *þīsl* 'thill.' Cf. § 83, 90, 4 N.

b) Foreign words were liable to dissimilation, thus *r — r* > *r — l*: Lat. *turtur* > OE. *turtur* and *turtle*, Lat. *purpura* > OE. *purpura* and *purple*.

e) METATHESIS.

61. Metathesis, or leaping, of sonorous cons⁸ is frequent, particularly: —

1) If thereby cons⁸ made with the same organs of speech are brought together: hros (Roß) > OE. hors *horse* § 69.

2) If thereby the sonorous cons. is brought near a more sonorous sound (§ 16, 3) than the one it has stood next: ādl > āld § 67, worsm > worms *pus*, tācn > tānc *token* § 74.

The metathesis of other cons⁸ is rare, cf. § 84.

CHAPTER VII.

Details as to OE. Consonants. §§ 62–91.

A. *The Semi-vowels* (w, j, § 16, 2).

w (cf. §§ 14, 15 & N³, 16, 2, 51; also 39, 45).

62. *Initial* **w** is often dropped after *n(e)* 'not': næs nǣron < ne wæs &c. *was not*; but it rounds *i* to *y*, § 17, 3: nyllan < ne willan *will not*. **w-** often falls away through weakness of stress in the second part of a compound: hlāford < *hlāfword, § 48.

63. *Medial* **w** falls away before the high vl' *u* and *i* (§§ 17, 2, 16, 2 about *w*): sǣ < saiwi *sea*; clēa < clāwu *claw* § 45, II, 1(1). Cf. also tū *two* < *twū < *twō (§ 33, 2), so hū *how*. But *w* is at times restored through the influence of forms without *u* or *i*: sǣw like gen. pl. sǣwa < sǣwja § 66 & N, &c.

64. *Final* **w** — 1) > vocalic, that is **u** (§ 16, 2): —

(1) After a cons.: barw(o)- > bearu *forest*.

(2) After a short vl., with which it forms a diphthong: *cnewo- > (§ 49) *cnew > *cneu > cnēo (§ 45, II, 1 (2)) *knee*.

2) Falls away entirely after long vl' and diphthongs: ā or ō < aiw *ever* (§ 35, 2), snā *snow*.

But *w* may be restored by analogy to medial forms: thus snāw like gen. snāwes.

j (cf. §§ 14 end, 16, 2, 55, 1, I. N, II. and 2, 56; also 40, 43, 45, 59, 1 & *b*.).

65. There was no special character to represent the semi-vowel **j** (= *y* in *you*); it was written —

I.) **i** sometimes (1) in foreign words: Iūdēas *jews*; (2) initially before the high vl. *u*: iung *young*; and (3) often after *r*: nerian *save*, § 59, 1 b, heries gen. of here *army*.

II.) **g** usually (§ 85): ġeong = iung, nęrġan = nęrian.

NOTE. — For *i* or *g* we sometimes find *ig* and before back vl⁸ even *ige* &c. (this may represent ï or ïj and in some cases even ī, rather than *j*): hęriġes, nęriġ(e)an.

66. j— 1) fell away after long closed slb⁸ saljan > (§ 59, 1 b) sęlljan > sęllan *give*.

NOTE. — As regards the interchange of *i* and *j*, — in G^c *i* + vl. stood after long vl⁸, and *j* + vl. after short: rīcio- OE. rīċe (§ 50 3 N¹) *realm* but racjan (OE. ręċċ(e)an, § 59, 1 b) *relate*. In OE. times the *i* too > *j* and fared as that did (for ex. *rīcies > *rīcjes > (§ 66) rīċes gen. of rīċe; *dōmian > *dōmjan > dēman *deem*); but, of course, it had not caused G^c gemination, § 59, 1 b.

2) was retained after **r** (nęrian *save*) and after a long open slb., § 19, (cīeġan *call*).

B. *The Sonorous Consonants* (r, l; m, n; § 20).

1. THE LIQUIDS (l, r).

l (cf. §§ 14, 16, 3, 20, **51**; also 41, 59, 1 c).

67. Metathesis (§ 61, 2) of **l** occasionally occurs: *sl* > *ls* in *brīdels* 'bridle' &c. (§ 98 *sla*); *spātl* later *spāld* 'spittle,' so *ādl* and *āld* 'sickness.' For *r* > *l* cf. § 60, II b.

r (cf. §§ 14, 15 N¹, 16, 3, 20, **51**; also 41, 57, 59, 1 c, 60 II b).

68. OE. **r** arises from —

I.) G^c **r**: bringan *bring*; wer *man*, Lat. *vir*.

II.) G^c **z**: māra *larger, more*, Goth. maiza; and cf. § 57 & N.

NOTE. — This *r* < *z* is only medial; for there was no G^c initial *z*, and the final *r* < *z* became silent: Goth. hwas wer OE. hwā *who*, Goth. batis OE. bęt *better*; Lat. hortus, Primitive G^c gardoz (§ 50, 3, I.) OE. ġeard *yard*.

69. Metathesis (§ 61) of **r** is common, especially if thereby the *r* comes to stand next other cons⁸ made with the tip of the tongue: hors *horse* Roß: beornan *burn* brennen.

DETAILS AS TO OE. CONSONANTS.

70. r is sometimes assimilated (§ 60, 1) to l and s: sēlra or sēlla *better*, lǣssa *less*.

71. r is sometimes lost after a labial: sprecan and specan *speak* ſpredjen.

2. The Nasals (m, n, ŋ).

72. Before the voiceless fricatives f, s, þ, a nasal early fell away and a preceding stressed vl. was lengthened: Goth. fimf fünf OE. fīf *five*, G^c gans > (§ 38, 1) OE. *gǫns > gōs *goose*, so mūð *mouth* Mund, *jugunþ- > ġeoguð *youth* Jugend.

NOTE 1.—Before the voiceless fricative h, the nasal had fallen out in G^c times: *þanhte > þōhte dadjte *thought*, cf. §§ 38, 1, 46, II.

NOTE 2.—After the working of the law stated in § 72, some nasals came to stand before fricatives in consequence of syncope &c. (clǣn(i)sīan *cleanse*), and some foreign words with ns &c. were brought in (pinsīan *weigh* < Lat. pensāre, § 38, 2)).

m (cf. §§ 14, 15 N[1], 20, **51**, 72; also 38).

73. For the metathesis of **m** cf. § 61, 2.

n (cf. 14, 15 N[1], 16, 3, 20, **53**; also 38, 88).

74. 1) Metathesis (§ 61, 2) of **n** occasionally occurs in the case of final *cn* and *gn*: tācn > tānc *token*, þeġn > þenġ *thane*.

2) **n** is often dropped in the pl. of verbs if *wē*, *ġē*, &c. follow (cf. § 82 N): *sohte ġē* but *ġē sohton* 'you sought.' Occasionally elsewhere: *cyning* > *cyn(i)g* 'king'; *onweġ* > *aweġ* 'away'; *nemnde* > *nemde* 'called.'

C. Non-Sonorous Consonants, § 20.
(p, b, f, v; t, d, þ, s; c, ċ, g, ġ, h, ḣ)

1. Labials, §§ 20, 2, 28, 2.
(p, b, f, v)

p (cf. §§ 14, 16, 20, **51**, 58).

75. Most G^c words beginning with **p** are words borrowed from other languages, § 11.

b (cf. §§ 14, 16, 20, 51, 58).

76. b generally represents the voiced labial stop (M^{n}E *b* in *bib*), but this only occurs initially (bindan *bind*), after *m* (limb), and doubled (habban *have*).

NOTE. 1. — Otherwise medially and finally we find **f** (often = r, § 52, 2) where we might expect **b**: webb (for web cf. § 59, 2 a) wefan *weave*, wæf *wove*. If foreign or initial *b* > medial, it, in time, > the voiced fricative **f**: Lat. probāre > OE. prōfian *prove, test* ; ā-byre *any time* > ǣfre *ever*.

NOTE 2. — In the oldest texts **b** is used to represent the voiced labial fricative afterwards represented by **f**: obaer = ofer *over*.

f (cf. §§ 14, 52, 76 N^{1,2}; also 58, 72).

77. f represents the denti-labial fricative (§ 20), both voiced and voiceless, § 52. Geminated voiced **f** appears as **bb**, § 76 N^1; for **b** = **f** = **v** cf. § 76 N^2.

NOTE. — Voiced **f** sometimes > **m** by assimilation to **n**: efne > emne *even(ly)*.

u or v.

78. Lat. **v** (or **u**) appears as **w** in the oldest loan-words (§ 11); but when it had become denti-labial in late Latin and the Romance languages, it was spelled **f** (fers *verse*) in OE., less often **u** or **v** (Dauid &c.), but this spelling became more frequent in time (uers *verse*).

2. DENTALS, § 20, 2.
(t, d, þ, s)

t (cf. §§ 14, 20, 51, 58).

79. t is sometimes lost, esp. (as generally in M^{n}E.) between a voiceless fricative and a sonorous cons. (rieh(t)liċe *right*, sōðfæs(t)nesse *truth*) or another fricative (Wes(t)seaxan).

NOTE. — (1) As sþ > st (§ 83) and the old spelling was often retained, we even find sþ written for original st: lǣsð = lǣst *least*. (2) As ċ had > tj or tʃ (§ 50 end) we also find the spelling c for original tj: orceard = ort-ġeard *orchard*.

DETAILS AS TO OE. CONSONANTS.

d (cf. §§ 14, 20, **51**; also 57, 58, 88).

80. Next voiceless cons', **d** > (§ 60) voiceless, or **t**, though the old spelling is often retained: bindst = bintst < bindest *bindest*, scencte < scenc-de *gave*, blēdsīan > blētsīan > blĕssīan *bless*. Weak *sind* (§§ 19, 3, 93 e) 'are' often > *sint*.

NOTE. — (1) For *ehte* < *eht-te* 'persecuted,' and *cyste* < *cyss-te* 'kissed,' cf. § 59, 2. (2) **d** often fell away between two l's: *siel(d)lić* 'strange.' (3) In weak slb' **d** fell away after **n** and before another cons.: *on(d)fōn* 'receive.' (4) Before l an **n** is often exploded as a **d**: *endlufon* Goth. *ain-lif* 'eleven.'

þ or **ð** (cf. §§ 14, 15 & N³, **52**; also 57, 58, 72).

81. The **þ** in old **lþ** and, after a long vl., **þl**, having > voiced, was stopped and exploded, that is, > **d**: Goth. gulþ OE. gold; Goth. nēþla OE. nǣdl *needle*.

82. d**þ** > t**þ** > tt, § 60: ēaðmōd *humble*, *ēaðmēdþu > ēað- mētto *humility*; þæt þe > þætte *that* conj.; and simplified, § 59, 2: bint < bintt < bintð < bindeð *bindeth*.

NOTE. — **þ** is often lost in verbs if *wē*, *ġē* follows (cf. § 74, 2): *binde ġē* but *ġē bindað* 'you bind'; also in *lār(ð)ēo* 'teacher,' &c.

83. s**þ** > **st**, that is, one of the two open cons' is stopped (§ 60, II): *hilpes þū* > *hilpestu* 'helpest thou,' the *t* in time being regarded as a part of the ending and remaining in *þū hilpest*; cf. also § 79 N¹. þs > ss: blīðs > bliss.

s (cf. §§ 14, 20, **52**; also 57, 58, 72, 83, 85, 3).

84. By metathesis (§ 61 end) **sc** sometimes > **cs**: āscīan ācsīan *ask*. Old **hs** in time > **cs** (§ 90, 4, N), and both this and other **cs**'s were very often written **x**: siex *six*, rīxīan *rule*, āxīan *ask*.

3. PALATALS AND GUTTURALS, § 20, 2.
(c, ċ, g, ġ, h, ḣ)

85. The original guttural cons' (**c, g, h**) became fronted (§ 20, 2) under certain conditions, but the Mss. do not generally distinguish the gutturals from the palatals. It is more or less customary in text books, esp. in the case of c and g, to place a dot, or some other mark, over the palatals.

1) c, g > ċ, ġ before the originally front vl' (æ ǣ, ea ēa, e ē, eo ēo, i ī) and their *i*-mutations (ę ǣ, ie īe, —, ie īe, —), but remained guttural before cons' and before the back vl' (a ǫ ā, o ō, u ū) and their *i*-mutations (ę ǣ, ę̄ ē, y ȳ), these last having become front vl' too late to affect the preceding cons. For examples, see Vocabulary.

2) Medial c, g > ċ, ġ before original i, j (cf. § 43 N¹): *bęnci- > bęnċ 'bench,' *bōcjōn- > bēċe 'beech,' *drūgi- > drȳġe, 'dry,' d. sg. byrġ < *burgi but d. pl. burgum, Lat. uncia > ynċe 'inch,' rīċe 'powerful, rich' and acc. sg. rīċne < *rīcina, similarly ēċnes 'eternity' as well as ēċe 'eternal.'

NOTE 1. — c was palatal also in īċ when final or before e: iċ 'I,' dīċ 'ditch,' -līċe '-like' (but -licor), and in the contracted derivatives in -līċ: ǣlċ 'each,' hwelċ 'which,' swelċ 'such.'

NOTE 2. — g was palatal also finally after the front vl' of monoslb' (dæġ 'day,' but dagas 'days,' &c.) and in the suffix -iġ (hāliġ 'holy'); and medially after front vl', provided no back vl. followed (dæġes 'day's,' lęġde 'laid,' þeġ(e)n 'thane,' but hāl(i)gu).

3) sc > sċ not only according to 1) and 2) above, but also initially (§ 11 d), and finally if no back vl. preceded (fisċ *fish*); in the latter cases it was the s that fronted the c. Where there was no front vl. next a medial or final sc, palatalization was delayed or prevented.

In the process of time, sċ > sċj > sċʧ > sʧ > ʃ, or the MⁿE. 'sh'; in OE. times it may have been at any one of the first stages. § 40 N³.

c (k, q; x) cf. §§ 14 end, 20, **56**; also 58, 85.

86. c is the letter most commonly used for both the palatal and the guttural voiceless stop, § 56; rarely the guttural was indicated by **k**: kyn(in)g *king*. In this book, the guttural is spelled **c**, and the palatal **ċ**. For the sound *kw*, the usual spelling was **cw**; in the oldest texts also **cu**, less often **qu**, as in Lat.: cwæð, cuæð, quæð *says*. For **x** = cs cf. § 84. For **ċġ** cf. § 55, 1, II.

DETAILS AS TO OE. CONSONANTS.

g (cf. §§ 14 end, 20, 55; also 57, 58, 59, 85).

87. After long back vl⁸, 1WS. h < g occasionally appears even in eWS., that is, final *g* tended to > voiceless: ġenōh = ġenōg *enough*; and rarely after **r, l**: burh = burg *fortress*.

88. After front vl⁸, ġ often disappears before **d, n**, but the preceding vl. > long: mæġden > mǣden *maiden*, breġdan > brēdan *pull*, briġdel > brīdel *bridle*, reġn > rēn *rain*, on-, tō- ġæġn > -ġǣn > -ġēan (§ 40, 1 b) *against*.

Note. — This loss of ġ is one of the proofs of the fact that even in eWS. medial and final ġ tended to become vocalic, or i̯.

h (cf. §§ 14, 15, 54; also 41, 45, 46 II, 57, 58, 87).

x (§ 84 end).

89. Initial **h** and often medial **h** acquired the weak sound that **h** has in MⁿE. (§ 54, 2), and in certain cases it was assimilated to neighboring voiced sounds or disappeared entirely.

90. h was retained when —

1) *Initial* (§ 89): habban *have*, hryċġ *ridge*.

Note. — Initial *h* is dropped when it comes to stand after another cons.: n(e)habban > nabban *have not*.

2) *Final*: furh *furrow*, wōh *bad*.

3) *Doubled*: hliehhan *laugh*.

4) Before a voiceless cons.: wiht *wight*, þohte *thought*, § 46 II.

Note. — For **hs** we often find *x*, and the fricative *h* in time > the back stop *c*, § 60 II.: siehs, siex *six*, weaxan *grow*. Rarely **h** fell away before **s**: þīsl < *þīhsl Deichsel *thill*, wæstm *growth*: weaxan.

91. h disappeared, with frequent lengthening of the preceding vl. (or assimilated to a neighboring sonorous sound), when —

1) Unstressed:

(I) fūrum < furhum d. pl. of furh *furrow*, befēolan < befeolhan *conceal*, būan < *būhon *dwell*, sēon < *sehon *see*, ēa < *ahwu *water*, § 45.

NOTE. — In WS. the loss of an *h* is often prevented by the early syncope of the following vl. (§ 50, 2 N⁸, § 90, 4), so esp. in the 3d sg. of the verb: **sihð* > Anglian *sið* but WS. *sihð* or *siehð* 'sees,' § 41, 3.

(II) Originally having secondary stress: *þūsund* < *þūs-hund* 'thousand'; names like *Ælfere* < *Ælf-here*; *-or(r)ettan* or *-ōrettan* < *-ōret* 'fight' < **or-hāt* &c.; *efen(n)ehð* 'level surface, field' < *efen-hēah* 'equally high'; *ǣǥðer* < *ǣȝhwæðer* 'either'; *on-hat'jan* > *onhęt'tan* > (by analogy to other verbs in unstressed *-ęttan*, § 94 b N) *on'hęttan* > *ōn'ęttan* 'hasten,' but *onhāt'jan* > *onhǣt'an* 'excite.'

NOTE. — The **h** is often maintained or restored by the influence of the stressed simple word, espec. if that have the same vl., § 95 c: *efenhēah*, 'evenly high,' but *efen(n)ehð* 'plain,' *ā'wēr* and *ā'hwēr* 'anywhere' < *hwǣr* 'where.'

2) Between a vl. and a voiced cons., esp. if sonorous, § 16, 3 : *smēalič* < **smeahlič* (§ 41, 3) < **smahlič* (§ 46, II.) <. **smāhlič* 'dainty,' so *nēawist* 'nearness,' *nēalǣcan* 'come near,' &c. < **nāhwist* &c. (*nēah* 'near' has *ēa* by analogy to these and to *nēar* 'nearer,' *nēan* 'from near,' § 45, 1 (1)), *lēoma* 'light' < **lēohma*, cf. *lēoht* 'light,' *wēofod* 'altar' < *wīh-bēod* 'sacred table,' *wō(h)dōm* 'false judgment'; *hēa(n)ne* acc. masc. of *hēah* 'high,' *nēa(r)ra* comp. of *nēah* 'near.' Occasional *hēahne* &c. are due to the influence of *hēah*, cf. note above.

CHAPTER VIII.

Stress.

A. *Sentence-Stress.*

92. A sentence involves the connection of two ideas: the one first in the mind is the **psychological subject**; and the one that attaches itself to this is the **psychological predicate**. These may or may not correspond with the grammatical subject and the grammatical predicate. If a theft has been spoken of and some one says "*John* stole it," 'stole it' is the psychological subject, and 'John' the psychological predicate; if John is under discussion and some one says "John is a good fellow," 'John' is the psychological subject, 'a good fellow' the psychological predicate, and 'is' a connective.

The psychological predicate is uppermost in the mind of the speaker, is the idea he is anxious to put into the mind of the listener, is the 'emphatic' word or words, and is, naturally, stressed.

93. 1) As a result of this, little stress falls upon words that refer to an idea already in mind (the psychological subject), and upon words that denote an idea that is necessarily or naturally associated with another and, consequently, neither excites the mind of the speaker or needs to be called to the attention of the listener, but is expected by him. Here belong words denoting only the relation ideas bear to one another.

Unstressed are, therefore: —

(a) Personal and relative pronouns (cf. e Note below).

(b) Weak demonstratives (including the article), which simply refer to objects in sight or under consideration (and do not contrast some with others).

NOTE. — Interrogative pronouns and adverbs, being but temporary symbols for unknown or undefined psychological predicates, are not stressed.

(c) Indefinite pronouns (mon, sum &c.).
(d) Most negatives and indefinite quantitative adj" and adv".
(e) Conjunc" and prep', copulative and auxiliary verbs, and verbs of saying &c. followed by þæt &c. (cwæð ꝥ, bæd ꝥ).

NOTE. — Prepositions are stressed before personal (but not demon.) pronouns and after nouns and pronouns.

2) The tendency to stress the psy. pred.,[1] when adapted to the primative word-order, gave to G^c speech a prevailingly trochaic rhythm[2] (using 'trochaic' in a broad sense): of two associated nouns (whether substantive or adjective) the first received the stronger stress — þæs **eorles** sunu 'the earl's son,' se **gōda** hierde 'the good shepherd,' **dēad** is Æschęre 'Æschere is dead,' — while a noun[3] was more heavily stressed than the verb with which it was used — **Bēowulf** maðelode, **bearn** Ęcgþēowes 'Bēowulf spake, the son of Ecgþēow,' — and this generally even if the verb was for any reason placed first — āhlēop þā se **gǫmela** 'then the old man leaped up,' but **gierede** hine Bēowulf 'Bēowulf prepared himself.' Like adj", adv" that retain a definite meaning have the heavier stress when preceding an adj. or verb — **bī** standan '*to stand by.*'

---

[1] It would not do to carry this matter into details here: suffice it to say that modifiers are degenerated psy. predicates, and that, when G^c speech was more synthetic, modifiers more regularly preceded the word modified.

[2] Through the operation of the same natural principle under changed conditions, — the more frequent use of proclitic words (prep", the articles, the auxiliary verbs, &c.) and the reduction or loss of final unstressed slb", — modern English has acquired a prevailingly iambic rhythm.

[3] In ordinary speech (where speech-laws originate) nouns generally represent psy. predicates, for they are usually displaced by pronouns when psy. subjects are to be referred to.

B. Word-Stress.

1. Chief Stress.

94. In OE. as in G^c

a) The stress of voice regularly fell upon the first[1] syllable of a word: SIMPLE, fæder *father*, þone *the*, clǣne *cleanly*, ġītsīan ġītsung *desire*, ċeorfan *cut*, monig *many*; COMPOUND, monslaga *manslaughter*, dōmsetl *judgment seat*, ārlēas *dishonorable*, blīðelīċe *gladly*, tōward *toward*. Cf. 2.

b) But COMPOUND VERBS stress the second member: —

    on-ġinnan *begin*, but on-ġin *beginning*,
    ā-cnāwan *know*,   "   or-cnǣwe *known*,
    tō-dǣlan *divide*,   "   tō-dāl *division*,
    wið-sacan *oppose*,   "   wiðer-saca *foe*.

NOTE. — Verbs with the derivative endings -lǣċan, -ettan, stress the first slb.: ānlǣċan *unite*, cohhettan *cough*.

c) Nouns (substantive or adjective) having the verbal prefixes *be-*, *ġe-*, *for-* also came (in OE. as in WG. generally) to stress the second member: be-hāt *pledge*, for-wyrd *destruction*, ġe-mǣne *common*, ġe-sihð *sight*.

NOTE. — The original prefix stress is still occasionally found (forwyrd, Crist 1615), and remained fixed in a few words, most of which early underwent contraction: bī-smer *disgrace*, *bī-hūt > bēot *boast*.

d) Derivatives retain the stress of the primative; thus, verbs derived from compound nouns keep the stress on the first member: andswarīan *to answer* (< andswaru *an answer*, not < and + swarīan); and nouns (for ex., participles used as adj^s or subs^s) keep the stress on the second member: ā-līesend *redeemer* and ā-līesednes *redemption* < ā-līesan *redeem*.

---

[1] In oldest G^c (§ 57 N), as in IE. speech, the accent was "free," that is, it was not bound by such a law; for ex., the word for 'father,' as in Greek, had the accent on the last slb. while that for 'mother' had it on the first, and the pret. pl. was not accented like the pret. sg.

e) Conglomerations generally retain the old sentence-stress (§§ 92, 93): tō-dæġ *to-day*, betwēonum *between*, for-þǣm-þe *because*.

2. Secondary Stress.

95. a) The second element of compound words (other than verbs, § 94, b) usually had secondary stress. For examples, see Vocabulary.

b) But when a compound in time assumed a simple meaning, there was a tendency to treat it as a simple word and to neglect the secondary stress; the second member was then exposed to all the changes suffered by unstressed sylb' (§§ 19, 3, 48–50, 91, 1, II): hlāf-weard > hlāford *lord*, ful-tēam > fultum *protection*, ā-hwǣr > āwēr *anywhere*.

c) Nevertheless, if the meaning of the second element of the compound was not entirely lost, the mental association of the simple word with it would maintain or restore the secondary stress in the compound, specially if both elements were long slb'; hence the rule a) above.

NOTE. — Of three more or less stressed slb*, the middle one was apt to lose its stress: ġehīer'sum'nes' > ġehīer'sumnes' *obedience*. Before a third slb. ′ ′ is apt to > ′ ′: Norþ'hym'bron, hund'twelf'tiġ = 120. It is generally not necessary to indicate secondary stress, unless it might be misplaced.

www.ingramcontent.com/pod-product-compliance
Lightning Source LLC
Chambersburg PA
CBHW031551110426
42739CB00039B/1364